Discover and Share

SEASONS

Angela Royston

FRANKLIN WATTS

LONDON•SYDNEY

About this book

The **Discover and Share** series enables young readers to read about familiar topics independently. The books are designed to build on children's existing knowledge while providing new information and vocabulary. By sharing this book, either with an adult or another child, young children can learn how to access information, build word recognition skills and develop reading confidence in an enjoyable way.

Reading tips

🌳 Begin by finding out what children already know about the topic. Encourage them to talk about it and take the opportunity to introduce vocabulary specific to the topic.

🌳 Each image is explained through two levels of text. Confident readers will be able to read the higher level text independently, while emerging readers can try reading the simpler sentences.

🌳 Check for understanding of any unfamiliar words and concepts. Inexperienced readers might need you to read some or all of the text to them. Encourage children to retell the information in their own words.

🌳 After you have explored the book together, try the quiz on page 22 to see what children can remember and to encourage further discussion.

Contents

What are the seasons? 4

Winter trees 6

Spring lambs 8

Chicks 10

Summer flowers 12

Hot sunshine 14

Autumn fruit 16

Falling leaves 18

Ready for winter 20

Quiz 22

Glossary 23

Index 24

Words in **bold** are in the glossary on page 23.

What are the seasons?

The seasons are the four different times of year – winter, spring, summer and autumn.

Winter is the coldest time of year. When we go outside, we wear a coat, a scarf and other warm clothes.

It is cold
in winter!
Put on your
warm scarf
and hat.

Winter trees

This tree has no leaves in winter.
In spring, new leaves will grow.

This is a branch
of an apple tree.
It looks bare in
winter, but there are
buds on the branch.

Inside each bud are tiny
leaves. They begin to grow
in spring, when the weather
gets warmer.

Spring lambs

During spring, the sunshine gets stronger and the weather gets warmer. Many animals give birth to babies.

Lambs are one of the first baby animals to be born in spring. Their woolly coats help to keep them warm.

Lambs are born in spring.
Their wool keeps them warm.

Chicks

Birds lay their eggs in **nests** in the spring. Chicks **hatch** from the eggs.

The parent birds catch food to feed the chicks until the chicks are old enough to fly away.

10

Chicks hatch in a nest.
Mum and Dad bring them food.

Summer flowers

Summer is the hottest season. Flowers grow well when the weather is warm and wet.

This flower is a poppy. It has four red **petals**. In summer, poppies grow along the side of country roads.

Flowers grow well in summer. Sun and rain help them grow.

Hot sunshine

In summer, the hot sunshine can burn your skin. You should put on sun cream.

Wear sunglasses, a sun hat and a shirt with long sleeves when you play outside. Drink lots of water!

The Sun is
hot in summer.
Rub on sun cream!

Autumn fruit

It is autumn and the weather is getting cooler. Many trees have **ripe** apples.

Each apple contains **seeds.** If the seeds are planted, they may grow into new plants next spring.

Apples are big and sweet in autumn. They have seeds inside.

Falling leaves

These are maple trees.
In autumn, their green
leaves change colour
to red and yellow
and slowly die.

The wind blows
the leaves and seeds
off the tree. The
seeds have wings
and they float away.

These leaves turn red in autumn.
Soon, they will fall off the tree.

Ready for winter

It is nearly winter again. There is still food for animals and they eat as much as they can before winter comes.

It is hard for animals to find food in winter. Squirrels **collect** and bury nuts in the ground to eat when the weather is cold.

Squirrels like nuts. They hide some nuts to eat in winter.

Quiz

1. What clothes are these children wearing to keep warm?

2. What are these chicks waiting for?

3. What happens to seeds when they are planted?

4. What is this squirrel doing?

Glossary

buds leaves or flowers before they open

collect pick up

hatch break out from inside an egg

nest place made by a bird to hold her eggs and chicks

petals colourful parts of a flower

ripe ready to eat

seeds parts of a plant that can grow into new plants

Index

apples 16–17
autumn 4, 16–17, 18–19

buds 7

chicks 10–11

flowers 12–13

lambs 8–9
leaves 18–19

nuts 20–21

rain 13

seasons 4
seeds 16–17, 18
spring 8–9, 10
squirrels 20–21
summer 12–13, 14–15
Sun 13, 14–15

warm clothes 4–5
winter 4–5, 6–7, 20, 21

First published in 2013 by
Franklin Watts
338 Euston Road
London
NW1 3BH

Franklin Watts Australia
Level 17/207 Kent Street
Sydney
NSW 2000

Copyright © Franklin Watts 2013

ISBN 978 1 4451 1733 1

Dewey number: 508.2

A CIP catalogue record for this book is
available from the British Library.

Series Editor: Julia Bird
Series Advisor: Karina Law
Series Design: Basement68

Picture credits: John L. Absner/Shutterstock: 10. Yuri Acurs/Shutterstock: 15.
blckwinkel/Alamy: 3t, 14. Paul Brough/Alamy: 21, 22br. Cheryl E. Davis /
Shutterstock: 11, 22bl. Dionisvera/Shutterstock: 1, 20. Wojciech Gajda/istockphoto:
front cover. gillmar/Shutterstock: 19 b/g. Herbert Kerher/Alamy: 3c, 6.
Liv friis-larsen/Shutterstock: 5. 1000 words/Shutterstock: 8. Neila/Shutterstock: 12.
Aton Prado Photo/Shutterstock: 16, 22cr. oliveromg/Shutterstock: 4, 22cl.
Zeijko Radojko/Shutterstock: 13. Annette Linnea Rasmussen/Shutterstock: 18b.
Rechitan Sorin/Shutterstock:9. swedewah/istockphoto: 3b. 19.
Visual Unlimited/Getty Images: 7. Valentyn Volkov/Shutterstock: 8, 17, 23b.

Printed in China

Franklin Watts is a division of
Hachette Children's Books,
an Hachette UK company.

www.hachette.co.uk